LIFE OPERATED FROM WITHIN

RAJDEEP UMESH

SCRIPTOR HOUSE
The Epitome of Greatness

Scriptor House LLC

2810 N Church St Wilmington, Delaware, 19802

www.scriptorhouse.com

Phone: +1302-205-2043

Published by Scriptor House LLC

Paperback ISBN: 979-8-88692-022-2

eBook ISBN: 979-8-88692-023-9

Contents

✧ Rendezvous with self ✧

Reet,on a lazy afternoon, is reminiscing his early days engrossed in a chain of deep thoughts, as he spins on the chair of his office cabin, looking over the streams of vehicles, as usual caught in congestion during the time of the day down the road, through the large window of a cozy and extravagantly decorated office environment on the fifteenth floor of the 'Wins Tower'.

Reet Ramesh is counted as one among the top-notch technocrats, engaged in an important role as solution provider for energy projects globally. Last week, he got nominated as President, responsible for global operations for his company.

Ten years earlier, when Reet was trying his luck to qualify a tender for his company as Contract Executive for his erstwhile employer in a competitive bidding process for a government project-enhancing energy storage capabilities , he had to cut a sorry figure for his company not qualifying in technical bid. On top of it, the mistake he made in mentioning the right technical specs in their offer, was cited as the reason for the rejection of the bid. Reet was reprimanded by his General Manager, for negligence, which he could have easily avoided if he were more vigilant. Reet had remembered the circumstances responsible for the mistakes, but this was not an easy excuse in presenting to the GM, Mr. Kalitta, as all these he could relate to his own personal anxieties on the penultimate day of bid submission. The last minute references to the web suggestions were not helpful to him either. In any case, he realized that this was no use in continuing any further with the organization, and he must resign before the suggestion reaches him to put down papers.

Reet calmly resigned from his job the next day and submitted his resignation to Mr. Kalitta at a critical juncture of his life when he was settled with his family in the south part of the city only two years back in the rented apartment with his four years old girl child and his wife over six years of wedlock. Mr. Kalitta seemed least bothered at the submission of the resignation, and he even felt no reason to utter any words, but his gesture explicitly implied his acceptance of Reet's resignation.

Reet was leaving the office in despair at the end of the day and met his peers to bid goodbye to all of them since he wasn't allowed to serve the notice period as conveyed to him by Mr. Kalitta in a message passed on by a messenger soon after he came out of Kallita's office. He also met the HR Administrator for her advice about his final settlement. HR Administrator told Reet that it should be followed as per the company's policy and procedures and would be communicated to him by email in due time. But all that, he must wait for the acceptance of his resignation by the higher management of the company. Reet was initially caught by surprise to hear that and wondering about how it was possible for Mr. Kalitta not allowing him to serve the notice period without the consent of the higher management. Although, in the end, this did not make any difference for Reet as he held himself responsible for the situation.

Afterward, Reet had no idea whether he would be able to secure a job in a short time or not. Nevertheless, he contacted as many of his well-wishers in person and over the phone as he could, and kept searching for a new job somehow to settle with. But this didn't appear easy for him to secure in a reasonably short time.

The other day, when Reet was aimlessly working on his laptop, his four-year old daughter had insisted on a new doll. After some time, Reet had overheard his wife Liza losing her cool and responding to their daughter Anaya in the harshest manner he had ever heard her doing so. This made Reet overtly restless as he knew that he had nothing much left in his bank account to sustain their needs and even the littlest demands of the child had cost their peace of mind. Poor little Anaya had no clue why her mother Liza seemed agitated lately. She cried and wept till she slept on her bed. Reet and Liza were caught in a serious altercation with each other over the issue after she slept. Reet had the opinion that it was not going to be the same story for over an abnormally long time. But Liza was in the opinion they couldn't hold it restfully, leaving it all up to hopes and Reet needs a serious job hunt within the next two to three months.

"Sir, should we book an appointment with Crystal Tech's representatives for a meeting next week?" The voice of Miss Teena was kind of a wake-up call as Reet came back to the present moment, realizing that he completely got lost in the past thoughts.

"Yes, Miss Teena, you may go ahead with scheduling a meeting after a couple of weeks of my travel planned over the next month to the South East," Reet replied promptly.

"Sure I would, Sir!" his personal secretary responded, and went out of the room with careful steps.

Reet could have realized that this is quite unconventional of his nature, as he had given up being driven by uncontrolled thoughts, long back. In no time, Reet restrained his senses and streamlined his clumsy thoughts to bring back his focus to the office organizer visiting his immediate agenda for the next week. He is of the opinion that one should check consistently the passing thoughts as those become the reality of the present circumstances, ingrained with emotions of the past events. "One must check his thoughts in real-time as thoughts are the reflectors of the present circumstances" The message once Reet received from Professor Krishnan, has been treasured for his lifetime. Reet met Professor Krishnan, while he was out of the job ten years before.

The morning after the day Reet had the serious altercation with his wife Liza ten years ago, he went driving down the road with multiple copies of his resume, visiting some offices he had known the locations of before. By afternoon, he was able to submit his application for suitable vacancies in three different organizations, including one government undertaking. Meantime, he felt like eating something out, and he entered one very popular outside food stall in the south part of the city. It was a brazenly cold day of December and Reet awaited little outside the place with the ordered food coupon held carefully in his hand. He was reminded of his former schoolmate Adi who was working in the design farm nearby. Reet checked in his mobile for Adi's contact, but he didn't find it on the list.

Reet observed a middle-aged person with a warm broad smile, clad with a blazer of pitch shade and costly sunglasses, approaching him from the other side of the crowd. The man proceeded to inquire him of an address. Reet was unprepared for the sudden approach by a stranger, but he answered him saying that he had no idea of the address after checking the same. However, Reet continued conversation with that person with a pleasant disposition, asking about what really had made him look out for the address since this address of the office was of some management school. The man introduced him as Professor G. Krishnan, and he spoke to Reet saying that he had been helping people to self-explore. And that day he had been invited as the guest lecturer at the school; however, he clarified that he didn't really do the job for any professional engagement or benefits, but for his sole agenda of helping people. The very introduction of the person had provoked Reet to inquire more about the stranger, but his ordered foods were already served on the table placed outside the stall. Reet just asked Professor Krishnan for his contact, and summed up by saying that he needed help from the professor. Professor Krishnan had given Reet his business card, promptly picking it out from his wallet. Reet thanked the professor with deep gratitude, shook hands, and went back to the food stall with a deep sense of contentment over the unanticipated yet sudden pleasant meeting with the person.

Reet arrived at home by evening. On his way, he had just bought the doll Anaya asked for. Strangely not like the previous day, his wife Liza was annoyed with the prevailing circumstances of their lives and even Anaya was in a far happier mood. Reet had handed over the toy to Anaya and this made her extremely happy. Liza seemed ok with the gift to Anaya, and she too didn't object this time.

That night, Reet suddenly remembered his conversation with Professor Krishnan, and he took out his business card to check his contact. Reet could read that Professor Krishnan had no office set up. He was living in the center of the city, not far from his apartment in the south. He called him on his mobile. Reet was a little nervous after dialing the number, but the familiar voice spoke from the other side with immediate response. Reet apologized to Professor Krishnan for the call at the odd hours and clarified that they met in the morning, and Krishnan acknowledged Reet with a comfortable response from the other end. Conver-sation went on and Reet learned that Professor Krishnan had a rich background in physics as an academician. Professor Krishnan retired only a couple of years ago, but he had something else to tell the people other than conventional science. Reet couldn't understand the brief of it, which he said, "Follow your impulses." Reet too had stated about the present circumstances that he was going through.

Professor Krishnan listened to him quietly with the utmost attention, and he responded to him after Reet had finished, asserting that nothing was wrong with the circumstances that he was through. But the professor said, "Reet, this is just the time you have to decide whether you want to go with how the situation is taking you through the ups and downs of life, or instead you wish to drive the circumstances yourself mustering your own potentials with a complete three-sixty degrees turn."

Reet couldn't understand the implications of his saying that to him.

The whole night, Reet was thinking about the conversation that he had with Professor Krishnan and was overwhelmed by something that literally he knew nothing about. He recalled Krishnan saying to him. "Young man, why do you wait for things to happen, why not master in materializing things you aspire for." Reet thought over, and he felt challenged by his logical inferences drawn from his own experiences. "You may aspire for anything, but would that be the sole reason for you to be able to materialize things in the manner you desire?" An unacceptable proposition for Reet in the current moment as life had shown up an ugly face to him just two weeks before. He was reminded of Professor Krishnan's conversations with him saying that, "To be able to succeed, discard the elements of doubt." Reet enquired to himself what he meant by saying so.

Reet was to meet Professor Krishnan the next day, as he really needed to know whether he had some tips for a way out from the present circumstances of the crisis. Maybe, Professor Krishnan had more insights on life tips that he would be able to share to get him out of the present situation. Reet spoke to himself why on earth he was interested in something about a strange discussion. Wouldn't it be more worthy to have searched for a few vacancies in companies by visiting personally instead of meeting Professor Krishnan? In any case, Reet couldn't resist the temptation of new concepts he might get to hear from Professor Krishnan and the next morning Reet drove to the professor's house.

Professor Krishnan had an impressive house and the security guard deployed at the gate had ushered him directly into the living room with nicely crafted wooden doors, windows, and furniture of intricate design. Reet could find ample space towards the front yard of the house with a mowed carpeted lawn extending all up to an outhouse near to the high compound wall. Reet had only seen this type of house in movies, and he started creating all crazy impressions about the person Krishnan, wondering what had made the person undertake the activities that he had been into, hailing from such a rich background. Reet considered himself to be just an ordinary person. How was it possible for Professor Krishnan to give him an appointment just in one single call? He should have many good reasons to avoid Reet.

Professor Krishnan clad in an overcoat greeted Reet after some time, and he took him straight to the lawn in the front yard. Reet felt a strange nervousness down his spine as he realized that this was something he was not prepared to face before he came to Krishnan's residence. Maybe every middle-class person would have thought it in the same way as he was thinking now, since Professor Krishnan was not from the class that he would normally interact with. Professor Krishnan had taken Reet for a walk just down the lawn. That was a relatively warmer Sunday, and Reet realized that the professor had no prior appointment with anybody other than him.

Professor Krishnan is obviously a pet lover, as he could guess from the variety of animal breeds he kept alongside the lawn as they moved on. Down the lawn were exotic flowers planted with the essence of multiple variations, reflecting the taste of Professor Krishnan. "Shall we have tea together, young man?" Reet hardly had any earlier opportunity in having tea on a lawn. Moreover, he wanted to experience the talks with Professor Krishnan as he felt that he had enormous wisdom in dealing with crises of life, which seem very unconventional of a person from Professor's background as most of the people belonging to this class seem careless about difficulties of middle-class people.

Reet eagerly looked up to the Professor to express what he was to say. Both had seated luxuriously on chairs under the lawn umbrella, and conversation went on endlessly.

This was the event of life that had entirely changed Reet for what he is now after ten years down the line, elevated to the position of President of a very prestigious company of energy solution providers across the globe from a very humble beginning as a contract engineer . Reet never dealt with Krishnan after he had met him the last on that day, and strangely it was no looking back for him to his past and in the want of Krishnan's suggestions thereafter, a result of the commitment of Reet to the request of Professor Krishnan.

When Reet came back home that day he was a totally changed man, enlightened with wisdom derived from the conversation that he had for about five hours at a stretch with Professor Krishnan. It was diametrically opposite to all lectures or discussions he earlier had listened to from any academicians and professionals. He recalled Professor Krishnan saying to him "Don't look out for outside factors attributing to the outcome affecting your state of being. Instead, feel the desired outcome emulated by your gross senses." In answer to Reet's query as to how this was possible, the professor responded, "Why did you resign from your job? You anticipated that you would be sacked, didn't you? You are pretty sure of your poor performance representing your skills in managing things. And that's where you are. You are a poor manager of yourself. If you are not convinced of yourself as a good performer, then how the other person would understand it from your behavior, which is the only means of signaling your potential to all others on this planet."

Reet again inquired, "But professor, how would you relate this to my mistake, which I already committed to quoting the right specification?" Krishnan said, "How do you know you made a mistake? A mistake only happens if it is discovered. Mistakes and non-mistakes have a very thin line." The professor laughed out loudly and continued his statement. "While you do things right, in order to avoid a mistake, you are bound to be caught up with mistakes. You are working out the mistake deep in your psyche, resulting from your habits in anticipation. You must stop anticipating mistakes, and instead you do things just as you think is right. To follow the right thing, you must engage your senses, emulating the state of achieving the desired outcome. Feel the accomplishment of the desired outcome using all your senses, I repeat using all your senses. Like how you would feel when you attain so-called success in a certain effort. Like that, you must follow the state of senses before attaining the objective, I mean the desired outcome."

Reet woke up early in the morning the following day before the other two members of the family. He just was seated in an old rocking chair oscillating leisurely on the balcony of his rented apartment with a deep inquiry down his psyche. He felt like not throwing up his frustrations, but accepted as they were. Furthermore, he dealt with each thought as those came through his psyche and responded to each of them consciously. He could discover that he was getting everything in his life as he had anticipated in the past. He even acknowledged the thoughts he had in anticipation of job loss, even though he didn't want it. He rechecked the reasons for anticipations as he could discover that this was due to his relentless habits of being prepared for the undesirable outcome from his school days like many other average kids. It was so deep-seated in his mentality, he could not just evade the likelihood of failing in the subject paper, not qualifying the interviews and many other undesirable events. He dealt with all intervening thoughts, witnessing from the roots.

He perhaps was never so fresh in his outlook and gratified with a deep sense of contentment without regrets of the past. He could see the sunrise, perhaps for the first time after so many years, with the aura of vermilion shade across the horizon. He just was gratified with something so ecstatic, with views of the sky to relieve all his stresses and regrets.

That afternoon, Reet when he was engaging his daughter Anaya for a game, withdrawing all his fear put aside gleefully for an unexplored unreal future with no specs of concerns and with conviction that he only had the quality time, meant to be spent with his daughter and to live up with the present moment.

Unexpectedly, Reet got to hear the caller tune off his phone. He recalled Krishnan's saying to him, "Don't create anything in anticipation out of the outside stimulant. Even if you think it is created by your habit, come back to your physical senses by settling down at yourself for a moment. Then respond to the outside call with complete awareness of your whole being. This imparts your control over the ongoing events." Reet followed accordingly, and realized that he needed to settle his own daughter first and said, "Anaya I have the call to attend." Which he meant by saying that to her, and he felt a complete sense of freedom in attending the call with no anticipation and with complete awareness of the impulses in his psyche.

Strangely, it was a call from Kallita, his GM in the former company. "Good afternoon, Reet. This is Kallita. Hope it is the right time to talk to you." Reet responded, "Yes Mr. Kallita, absolutely no problem, I am at home and free from any engagements." "Reet, your resignation was not accepted as advised by the company president . You need to report urgently to the office tomorrow." The voice from the other end further said, "Just for your information, our technical bid is further revisited by the Government Tender Committee. They found it most suitable for their requirements. Commercial evaluation is still ongoing, and we hopefully would qualify for the same in a day or two. Reet, we almost have done it for a very prestigious award of a contract by the government, and the Board of Directors have recommended even for your promotion as the Senior Executive-Contract." Reet had no idea how the transformation of the same event had happened from the worst to the best, but he followed his own impulses closely in response to the communication by Mr. Kallita, restfully drawn with complete awareness of the circumstances that he was experiencing throughout the call over the real-time.

Reet thanked Mr. Kallita, saying to him that he would report to the office the next morning. Reet could follow his emotions resulting from subtle work in overcoming the crisis which he earlier had regarded as the worst event for so many days over the last couple of weeks. He dealt with each thought that he was through that moment after the call and just not letting it at a loss to the state of being overjoyed, or even to the state of despair.

Reet could recall that his quote of the technical specs was not matching the tender document, since they didn't have the right material. So, he referred to his former colleague, Ryan. Ryan had given him a tip for a request in changing the specs to the principal employer followed by an amendment, but Reet couldn't seek to discuss with his superiors about the matter since he thought this should have been taken up at the right time instead of taking up the matter at the eleventh hour. Moreover, Reet considered the quoted specs more appropriate to what was mentioned in the tender document. Reet went ahead in quoting the specs by his own choice, which turned out to be history for his company, full of events over the last couple of weeks right from his resignation to the awarding of the contract, including his rejoining in a promoted position.

"History may be amended.". He remembered Professor Krishnan saying this to him the previous day. When Reet asked why that should be, Krishnan said, "It is a matter of perception when somebody holds back in his eyes on the past events regarded as unchangeable. But what anybody sees is only the partial side of the past event, a person narrates as he sees the event as. But there are many other sides of the same story." Professor further stated, "When it is somebody who lands up in troubles, the troubles that do not really exist in outside events, but it is in anticipation of his own troubles led by events. So, one must aspire for the desired outcome that you are comfortable with, even if you don't see the right reasons for that, but you need to keep aspiring. With this effort, the same past event, which you once despaired at, would be a total change and would be entirely meaningful for you. You must make it a point not to be caught up with vibes of the undesired outcomes of the event with your nagging habits of anticipating the worst, but to aspire for the desired outcome. This can only be accomplished if you follow your pattern of thoughts with total honesty."

Reet recalled and consumed the answer from Professor Krishnan about when he put the query about what is anticipation and aspiration, "Reet you must know the mechanics of the acquired habits which essentially have deep impacts on outer happenings. Every time you experience something some way or another way round, you acquire the essence of experiences in terms of memories. Accumulation of memories deep-seated in your mind forms impressions about persons, living things, and even materials. It carries impressions about your identity based on your opinion and others. So, your every action is guided by the impression you already have about things in the surroundings and even about your potential. You anticipate things which you think you already have experienced. That's why there is rapid growth in the children acquiring new qualities as they do not anticipate much due to lack of any prior experiences. But an average adult is just preoccupied with earlier experiences, which they associate with any new tasks they do. Experiences of any failures would bring forth the taste of failure in new tasks as a result of anticipation. That's how you fall into a vicious cycle of failures all through. You must have seen the rich becoming richer and the poor becoming poorer, with a very clear indication of using their experiences by default. Just to be able to come out of the complexities of this kind of situation, one must have to aspire for all new experiences using experiences of successes that the person must have had earlier at some point of time in his life. To dispense the experiences of success, you must use physical senses aligned and prepared. Like you must have to feel the same way if you were attaining success in achieving the objective of your task. You don't have much to do with processes to accomplish a task. The manner if you aspire like that your action would automatically follow the right processes to achieve the objective. If you are to climb up the mountain to the top, you gather the fulfillment of your ideas in landing up on top of the mountain, engaging all your senses and emulating the experiences. The process would certainly follow all your actions in reality needed for the accomplishment of the objective just in a matter of reasonable time. This is how aspiration helps to achieve.``

The next morning, Reet joined the office and was greeted with a warm welcome from his peer group and his boss. He straight went down to his cubicle and realized the worth of a job after a brief celebration with the cutting of the cake. In the cubicle, he was reminded of the hug from his wife Liza when he passed on the information to her for rejoining the office the next day, an emotional moment worth cherishing for the whole of his lifetime.

Reet knew that he had committed Professor Krishnan not to look out for him again ever after their last meeting . Professor told him that day, "Young man, I am not your mentor. Not even a so-called guru. I am showing you a path forward, but remember that you are not the only one on this planet needing guidance. I do it for a single person in a day and do not keep any connections afterward after a meeting. I also request you not to be in touch with me for any help after this day. Furthermore, I just have reminded you of your potential and the rest is up to you to explore on your own."

There was no looking back for Reet in fulfillment of his aspired thoughts for the rest of his life after his rendezvous with himself, as introduced to him by Professor Krishnan, once and forever.

✧ The Inner Etheric Space of Consciousness ✧

Amid the backdrop of certain directives, which need not necessarily be outer factors but sometimes may also be inner, Reet starts thinking of writing his experiences and the wisdom he acquired over time. A subtle decision of the psyche triggers a thought in his mind, and he now aspires to accomplish something for fulfillment But the necessary materials have not yet appeared at the forefront of Reet for finishing his intended piece of work.

Slowly, Reet started looking around to derive materials from the accumulated stores of memory with the chain of thoughts knocking at each cell of his physical presence, causing these to be activated. A direction starts appearing in his mind, emanating from the source in the vortex of his psyche. The accumulated memories of Reet associated with words and with sounds, sights, and information from all his senses have paved a way for his writing. The rules are all in play and synched with the action of his writing to the rhythm of the chain of thoughts as they come through like water from a flowing river, its source to the sea.

Reet's actions over a definite time span have become a series of small acts stimulated by thoughts with aid of discrete memories, associated by virtue of logic and inference that have started materializing in this written piece of Reet. Reet is in the opinion that this is like what conventionally happens in our day-to-day lives in managing our way of life.

Regardless of anything, we human beings are driven by our experiences , including those which are very recent, from the register of our memories. We are stimulated by an object, irrespective of its place in the outer domain or our inner psyche. A decision, a subtle definitive act of the mind based on the accumulated memories, triggers an action, be it an expression or anything sensible, which results in another activity of experiencing things and registering these in the memory.

This is, however, sensed as a repetitive, cyclic, and monotonous process, though it comprises discreetly different pieces of each event that are associated qualitatively. According to Reet, we generate our memories in a reactive process, but this can be translated into a creative process. If we follow closely the process of our conventional activities, we will see that these are more spontaneous sets of actions in response to the experiences triggered by our thoughts. But by delinking the stored memories with pauses, which are borne by each cell of our physical being, we can make the event a creative one, far different from the conventional sequence of the event. There exists a gap between each thought,which is the space of creation, unbiased towards any stimulus in the outer domain, and the register of inner functionalities.

Since we don't assign importance to the gap of thoughtlessness, it produces the materials of the event reactively, in response to earlier experiences, and is, therefore, not felt as any different in terms of using these experiences. But according to Reet, if we can own the space that appears after every stimulus which triggers the thoughts and can start living in that space, then we forge a new virtue and start creating events with our determination. In this way, life becomes more creative, and a higher quality of substances is brought forth into our lives. This may seem a bit unconventional, but it helps to keep us on the right track and to use the non-judgmental, no illusive, etheric space of our consciousness.

Nevertheless, Reet opines that this is a solid state of one's being, determining the quality of one's life by surrendering to the inner space in the light of one's experiences. For an individual, the act of holding back to preserve his image, or anybody else's image, usually is the result of what is borne in packages of the person's thoughts. Thoughts are not necessarily embedded in a continuous format; they are all discrete and separate. Thoughts are realized as an event in the mental realm when they pop up in a chain in a quick interval after the gap in etheric space where each thought pauses. So, a person preserves his image in identical thought capsules connected by etheric space, which is completely free of the images that we all tend to carry in preceding and subsequent thoughts.

Ideally, successive thoughts are the carriers of the preceding thoughts and all their qualities, as these are reactively produced by the process. But etheric space is a neutral creator of the materials which largely berth random thoughts in the mental domain. We sense a nagging feeling about the events in our lives when we fail to rely on dimensionless etheric space and our thoughts function perpetually without the realization of the pause.

The pause is not an established act of stopping our thoughts but is an art of withdrawing from thought functioning while neutralizing the traits of doer-ship for any intended piece of work.

According to Reet, his life and all its events are carried by his thoughts in modules that are embedded in nondimensional etheric space, the sole characteristic of consciousness. He considers that consciousness is the reflector of everything produced while we are experiencing events. To be more precise, the role of awareness, also called consciousness, is just like the function of a mirror, which reflects all things in this world barring itself. And Reet further says that material entities are the precipitation of thoughts as the result of our thoughts' reflections on the surface of the etheric mirror of the consciousness.

✦ Amendable History ✦

"Reet, all the oil tanks are showing no level indication in the control room," said a murmuring voice through his handheld phone. Reet naturally was dumbstruck for a moment as this situation could lead to big trouble with the oil terminal that he was heading up with the bare minimum of resources in hand after he rejoined his former company after the incident of his resignation. Meantime, he was given the task of quickly fixing a loss-making unit of the company located in a remote location.

At the moment, Reet could feel that it was not a desirable situation but, accepting the situation, he responded the very next moment: "I'll be right there. No worries. It will be taken care of." But Reet really didn't have the slightest idea how. Within five minutes, he arrived at the control room, a little distance from his office, and found that the problem was a damaged rectifier in the uninterrupted power supply. It would take at minimum two months lead time to procure the component if he were to order it. So, no option was left for leaving it to any human intervention, and for him, it was just a passing incident bound by an unprecedented set of conditions that he had to experience in any case without hopes or distress. Reet was simply the witness to the moment. Not really trying to figure out any of the potential consequences of drawing the tentacles of his physical senses in anticipation within himself, coupled with an aspiration to see things fall into place on their own. A moment later, he heard a loud voice rise from those gathered, saying, "Could this help, Reet?" The person who'd asked this question showed him a similar model rectifier unit. Reet spontaneously replied, "It could." He let out a large sigh of relief as the rectifier was fitted in place to restore the plant to normal functioning. This was not the only occasion where he had literally felt helpless, boxed in on all sides, and where, refraining from doing something in anticipation and acting out of his doer-ship based on experiences, he left things as they were to be inwardly managed by his psyche. When Reet, according to his inquisitively logical nature, enquired about the rectifier, his teammate said that this component had been left in the storeroom as a spare a long time ago by the vendor. He mentions this to prevent you from being caught by surprise; things have their own history, contrary to the seemingly magical appearance of the rectifier emerging at the instance when it was needed. But that very emergence was apparent with its presence at the moment, whereas history, the object's background, may be retrieved with no tangible traits.

As a matter of fact, this idea causes us to vacillate between the choice of whether to allow for materialization at the moment based on the logical inference of the object's history, where history can never change to suit our strong logical perception or to seek to mend the moment with ideas reinforced in our psyche as amendable history. The job of the psyche is to connect every single present moment to produce an event, ideally backed up by experiences . But present experiences, if they are independent of the past, can cause any story to turn into a saga of creativity where the stubborn pattern of history also changes subjectively.

Reet further discusses the topics as would follow in this book after this, for readers to be enlightened with the very concept of "life operated from within", which he recommends for anybody on this planet irrespective of his or her age, gender, profession, and the hobbies to be guided steadily and consistently.

✦ Ample Opportunities ✦

We human beings have attained a level of civilization in which we have realized almost all our past dreams and have never looked back. In our quest, with all our inquisitive rationales, we have traveled many miles while exploring this mysterious world and have seemingly grown more and more curious and become more experimental, hoping to quench the thirst brought on by our intrusive mind blocks. But this in and of itself appears to be an endless process. All discoveries and inventions, arising as they have from necessity, are the result of our inclination towards the fulfillment of our human desires. But here we may question whether these are creations borne of the needs of the majority of people or borne of the creativity of the experiments performed by a few individuals. Reet suggests asking ourselves if we are not really reconstructing things that are already around us. Is it not that we're coming of ourselves and making things, according to our tastes, out of the existing opportunities that are already available in the environment in which we dwell?

The universe that we see around us, above and beyond the foundation of our consciousness, affords ample opportunities for us to create things that we would like to create but that we have not really been aware of.

Sometimes we reel within a vicious cycle of misery and cannot conceive of the slightest idea of how to get out of this predicament and make things for ourselves. We marvel at human ingenuity, having broken all barriers, but the world is still struggling to combat the miseries experienced by most of humankind. Are we not required to understand how we can benefit ourselves with the opportunities afforded by the environment?

To appreciate the world around us, reflected from the surface of our consciousness, we must abandon the conventional set of beliefs that we have been nurturing for so long and become totally convinced that we are born into this world to be happy and blissful and that we may avail ourselves of all possible opportunities to create things for ourselves. Can you imagine a world without sorrow and grief, without ailments, without poverty, without violence, without disputes? Can you imagine a world where you have everything that you wish to achieve? Yes, we have taken a giant leap on our way to becoming more evolved creatures which in no time shall become aware of our hidden potential, our sheer power, by which they shall be able to materialize all their needs from the abundant non depleting sources of the universe residing in the inner etheric space of individual consciousness.

According to Reet, the time has come when we all must be unified with the greater self to be able to tap into the inexhaustible resources of the environment that surrounds us. If we closely observe human beings as well as other forms of life on earth, we cannot deny that they all are creators themselves. But we need to give ourselves a little space to understand this fact.

A small example can be given along these lines, namely that an animal can create its own progeny equipped with physical bodies, the sort of machines that even the greatest human scientist would not dare to claim to be able to create artificially. Just consider where the power to create such a complex organism has come from. We are so used to regarding many such instances as normal because we are bogged down by the monotony of the series of events without looking into the inner creative space of our own consciousness.

✦ Humans as Creators ✦

We see the creations of human beings in all spheres of life and yet are not fully convinced that we are part of the very process of creation. For anything you see around you, you have contributed to the process of its materialization. According to Reet, the time has come for all of us to become aware of this fact, or else we will never know about that within us that has consistently contributed by playing its role in each event we have come across. In all cases, if something good has happened to us, we have created it, and if anything bad has happened to us, we unknowingly have caused it to materialize in our lives. The whole saga of good and bad is our creation at the individual level. And essentially, we have the potential to change things. The environment that we dwell in forms an integral part of our entity. Reet suggests that for him to elaborate on the matter, we need to understand that whatever we see in the outside world is happening within the domain of our consciousness. But constrained by nature, the ordinary human being senses that his feelings are all that is happening on their own, largely attributable to his historical background, and on the individual level he feels he has very little control over his emotions. This prevailing notion among most people, Reet says, has been the sole barrier to our becoming happy and successful in our efforts.

Reet asks the readers something. Do we believe that anything we may hear around us is being reproduced by the integral audio sensory parts of our bodies, imparting an individual sensation to us? Aren't we creating the effects if we compare the phenomenon of sound to what happens to a hearing-impaired man? Given the same factor in the outside world, there are two separate effects for two separate individuals. And the components responsible for this are none other than our human organs, which impart the sensation to our physical senses. This matter becomes more interesting if we are talking about our sense of vision. Reet beg pardon for posing the hypothetical of a man who is blind in one eye and unfortunately cannot view movies with three-dimensional effects, thereby ruling out the possibility that the scientific phenomenon of three-dimensional planes will permeate his level of understanding if he has been blind since birth. To be more precise, the man who is blind in one eye would view all objects in the movie as reflected in normal two-dimensional cinematography. Reet's point here is not to give you the hypothetical situation of the man who is blind in one eye and the man who is deaf to discuss their disabilities, but to illustrate the utility of the human body as the tool that creates effects that we presume to be happening outside our bodies. When we close one eye, we see things in two dimensions in a movie through the goggles, and when we open both eyes, we see them in three dimensions. Is the environment of the movie with its screen before us responsible for this, or are we responsible for it?

And in a bid to be one step ahead, Reet inquires that have we ever thought of the viewer who uses the tool of her body to perceive the world or rather to create the world for herself using all the sensory organs? Matters may be defined as the substances generated by the consolidation of all the senses based on the observer's understanding and experiences within the framework of a single plane of consciousness. The transitional changes of matter in shape and form in a certain configuration vis-à-vis physical time make it possible that a series of events will occur, and these are essentially the function of our physical senses and so, in turn, are the function of consciousness. However, in this regard, a person may claim that nothing is created on the level of consciousness but is rather happening outside, which factors in the effects as perceived by our senses. To better understand this, consider dreams, which are a creation of the subconscious brain. We tend to perceive them as outside events occurring spontaneously. In the process, we can hardly keep track of the pace of our creative selves while creating the events within our consciousness and instantly projecting them as outside factors. We interact with other entities often in dreams, but these so-called other entities are nothing other than our own creation in our dreams. We see a similar kind of action, but the only difference between a dream and reality is that the former consists of subtler events than the latter. Reality is grosser with its inherent characteristic of qualitative repetitiveness of events in nature due to the perceptions carried by consecutive sequential thoughts. We have come to see ourselves as having a consciousness influenced by the sensory organs of our material bodies that are interacting with the material world, forgetting the creative side of our consciousness. Let this discussion help you understand how we are born into this world. It may be supposed that you believe in the role of the incorporeal form of the consciousness and that it is the consciousness that creates the corporeal form of the self on the mental plane.

Once we are conceived in our mother's womb, we start creating material envelopes around us using our mental tools. In our mother's womb, the material envelopes are made up of our own physical body and the uterine environment surrounding the fetus. Just think that human progeny is in such a powerful state of being during this time. The mother's mammary glands also start gradually producing milk to prepare for the child's nutrition when it is born at some later point. However, when we are born, we soon start creating our physical bodies for sustainable growth to create the outside world's environment. As things in the outside environment of the body take shape in the form of matter and events, and as we gradually adapt by consolidating our senses with changes in the forms perceived by our thoughts, we tend to react to those things with the presumption that they are inflicted by outside forces. Our consciousness tends to deal with these virtual outside forces and leads us to create more of such matter and events in a relatively uncontrolled manner without our active attention and with the belief that all these things are happening on their own, caused by outside factors, and that we at the individual level have very little control over these events and the materialization process. This phenomenon becomes more complex when an individual creates his helplessness without his knowledge.

✦ Types of Material Envelopes ✦

The material envelopes, as Reet explains, in the foregoing chapter may be classified into two types to make it easier for us to understand: the primary material envelope and the secondary material envelope. The primary material envelope is the physical form of the body, and the secondary material envelope is the material environment around the physical body. The basic difference between the two is that an individual assumes that she has more control over the primary envelope than she has over the secondary envelope. But as a matter of fact, an individual has either control over both or control over neither. The key to a person's success is that she does not differentiate between the two, and that she holds herself fully accountable for whatever she has produced for herself. As explained earlier by Reet, we reproduce outside effects employing the sensory organs of our physical bodies within the domain of our consciousness. In other words, the secondary envelope resides within the primary material envelope, allowing us to have similar control over the outside world as we have over our physical body. And this awareness within us allows us to produce the so-called outside events according to our own choice and will. In this process, the entities of our consciousness develop certain subtle characteristics within the mental domain such as intelligence, along with impressions, behaviors, and more importantly inculcated habits, which we know as the various forms of thought, while dealing with these material envelopes from within. These characteristics, even though they appear to be separate characters, are nothing but forms of our unique consciousness. Likewise, all the body's senses are subtler, borne by the mind, and are nothing other than different forms of the same unique consciousness. Hence, it is easier to understand that material envelopes are the function of one's consciousness. So why shouldn't we take full control of our consciousness and guide our destiny, which we have been convinced for a very long time has been in the hands of so-called outside forces. The moment we consciously become one with the outside world, we come closer to the greater force responsible for whatever is happening to us, imparting to us the leverage to make things aligned with the way we choose them to be. Just as Reet reminds us that this happens not by way of wishing, but by accepting that all things are forms and elements of our own individual consciousness instead of separate identities. This provides us relief from the struggle to identify a great many things with ourselves at the level of individual consciousness. All he has explained above is only an attempt to make you understand the role of this greater force and the potential of our individual capabilities working hand in hand with the greater force, one part of the whole. In practice, he suggests bringing this realization to your consciousness and making full use of your potential, you must devote yourself to engaging in certain exercises. Since knowledge plays a very important role in the process of our transition towards becoming more evolved human beings, Reet further discusses some issues which we are already familiar with but which we have never thought about with the depth that such issues deserve.

✦ Light: Color of the Consciousness ✦

All objects in this world are essentially light. We perceive matter in the form of light; however, the phenomenon of the things we perceive is the result of the reflection of the objects' photons moving through the retina. Imagine that wholeness has no meaning without perception and that the mind, being the processor of perception, must deal with light to bring clarity to existence. All our bodily senses are elaborate expressions of light if we look at them closely. For simplification purposes, if we hear a sound echoing in some corner, we can make out its location within the surrounding space with the anticipation that it is an object creating the sonorous effect. On the other hand, both objects and space are nothing more than functions of light. If we are speaking of the mind, we always comprehend the subtler visuals, and visuals are essentially light. So, as with all senses, they are meant for the light. The light in a physical sense that is perceivable by our eyes and the light we create by way of visualization, though, are apparently different from each other. But both are the functions of consciousness essentially meant for each of the categories of said uses. Light in a pure context is all things in the universe and the play of consciousness. Understanding this is the key to the evolution of humankind and to the conversion of that which is perceptible into a creation. The creation of that which is perceptible to the senses precipitates the materialization of worldly objects. The case could just as well be the other way around, as conventionally worldly objects are perceptible to the senses, which are responsible for the creation in the form of change. Light again is a delight aspired to by the consciousness. Consciousness grows with light from a state of inertness, a state closer to a condition without light. The use of the eyes of consciousness is instrumental in the creation of light in the form of all matter and objects within the universe. The corporeal form of the self is also a form of light and is essentially a tool to bring forth the light in diverse forms and shapes, essentially to create and possibly to enable the interaction of consciousness among multiple entities guided by the mechanism of duality. Duality is the process of disintegration of self into multiples at the conscious level. This will be discussed later. To realize the nonduality factor is to interpret everything perceptible as being the light of a single consciousness. Transcendence of the consciousness is possible if we closely follow the light in action over all earthly realities within the domain of the consciousness that we are subjected to. Light is the ultimate state of consciousness and, concerning all its existing metaphors, can be invoked for its persistence in the worldly environment that we dwell in, in our domain of consciousness.

✦ Matter versus Spirit ✦

A human form is seen to be a metaphor for matter and spirit. In trying to understand the spirit, one should not misinterpret it as the energy available in the physical sense like that of forces that are predominant in the outer environment backed by scientific logical inferences of their material origins. The spirit that is spoken of here is consciousness manifested through our entities. The form of energy spoken of here is the type that we spontaneously witness as the movement of light through our senses in different forms. In all our interactions with the material environment, we are interacting with energy through matter perceived by the mind on the mental plane, the manifestation of spirit at the gross level, which has a high degree of inertia towards its expression. If we consider the pure form of the spirit for its extraordinarily high dynamics, the matter would be just the opposite, highly inert because of the characteristics of obstinate impressions carried by thought. The different strata of the self are an expression of the dynamics of the pure form of spirit, converted in stages into the matter that is encapsulated in thoughts that pause over the etheric environment of the consciousness with its explicit expression in the gross form. The physical body is the representation of the gross level of our manifestation, followed by a subtler level of energy in the form of vital attributes like physical strength; an even subtler form such as the mind; and even the subtler the intellect, the carrier of the information guiding the mind; and even subtler the self, created beyond the body, mind, and intellect, all of which we bear in the name of the representation of ourselves. An individual may become attached to a certain stratum of his manifestation, the place where he chooses to dwell, and therefore the movement of the consciousness within this boundary is constrained by the limitations of the image that he creates for himself using the mental plane, which in turn is an elaborate function of thought embedded in the etheric space of consciousness. A normal person through her attachment to a form and identity tries to comprehend her existence, which in most cases is more physical and which therefore becomes the explicit expression of her relationship with matter. The cycles of the manifestation of the consciousness from the stage of gross matter to the purest form are the movement with the light. If we are faced towards the light, we won't be facing the resultant shadow. The practice of facing the light would mean one is centered in the pure form of the self, which opposes the material self. While one is centered on one's material self, it causes all sorts of friction with existence because of the presence of inertia. It is not always the case that one's life is devoid of all kinds of material attributes if one chooses to be centered on his spirit. On the contrary, this would greatly multiply one's pleasure when dealing with the material environment. This pleasure would manifest in the form of sheer bliss, and accomplishment would be driven only by spontaneity. In our dealings with the types of material envelopes we have discussed, we must be centered on our form as an abundant source of energy in inner space, and translate the actions in the material environment through the creative process instead of through reaction.

✦ The Fourth Dimension of Consciousness ✦

When we bring something close to our eyes, we tend to see it physically with a certain outline, but in our mind we don't see the same thing identically outlined. The gross elements of our perception with the physical eyes are those objects defined by the dimensions, but the impressions we carry in our minds are not necessarily defined precisely by the dimensions. Our perception in this case is just the product of our feelings or emotions carried by our thoughts in the mental plane beyond the dimensional environment; perceived by our physical senses; and extending up to the level of our state of being in response to the physical appearance of the objects or living things we deal with in the time. We constantly drag into our minds all the external factors, which are not similar in physical appearance to gross reality. Hence, the environment we create around us is just that which we perceive through our physical senses, and more precisely, with a blend of our thoughts and impressions arising out of our accumulated experiences in response to the physical appearance of the material substances. When we see an object or a living thing for the first time, we start creating our impression through personal judgments in our bid for familiarization, and these impressions are carried along in our mind with the creation of more diverse impressions arising from our subsequent real-time interactions with the object or the living thing. We bear all our impressions in a dimensionless environment, and the situations we go through are all on account of the impressions we harbor in our state of consciousness. In meditative practice, the divine light people proclaim to see is not light perceived by the physical eyes. Rather, it refers to a blissful state of delight in the consciousness interacting with the inner state of being in a timeless and dimensionless environment. It is the light perceived beyond the eyes and all physical senses. This state is so highly ecstatic and so highly powerful, much more powerful than the state of an individual ego centered on the primary material envelope, that we become assimilated with the inner space, losing all our entities. And if we maintain this state when we interact with objects and living things in the worldly environment, our state of being becomes the witness to all actions performed at the individual level. This realization begins bringing us to a place of self-awareness, identifying the pure form of consciousness separate from the individual entity, which is not engrossed in the state of individuality. Thus, the concept of the three dimensions adds to the fourth dimension. The physical eyes, which are capable of viewing things from a three-dimensional perspective, again are witnessed by the entity from within and from the fourth-dimensional plane, leveraging absolute control over our state and fate itself. There is a created self in the context of individual consciousness, which is factored by the chain reactions that occur in response to the environment we constantly create for ourselves. When our individual entities are deeply engrossed with the environment that we deal with, we tend to forget the aspect of the fourth dimension berthing the creator within us, and actions that we take seem to be unwise. When we witness our actions in real-time in the physical environment from the perspective of the fourth dimension, situations that we are going through seem to be far easier and more relaxed. This fourth-dimensional perspective of visualization is what the human being must become aware of to gain the ability to witness her thoughts and actions from a non-judgmental perspective over the inner space. Once this is attained, humankind will evolve, which is overdue. However, when one remains a witness to the surrounding things in the material environment, he finds that such an environment includes not only material substances perceived by the physical senses, but also essentially his state of consciousness with all kinds of forces present within its domain being assessed in the present moment by the self from within. The practice of witnessing the forces in action within and outside the domain of the consciousness in a non-judgmental way brings inherent value to our existence. Exercising this technique leads us to a state of blissfulness, untouched by materialistic troubles, where we find that the marvels of the forces witnessed by the conscious entity are seated deep within the inner etheric space.

✦ Theory of Eternity/ Eternal Existence ✦

This chapter is an effort for Reet to establish the fact that the existence of the self is eternal. He explains that the most persuasive piece of evidence for this is the point of an individual's self-realization, which leads to the understanding that we all happen to coexist in living form (or in transitional non-living form) at this very moment. He further explains that the mathematical representation of this theory could be helpful to our understanding if we were to find that the probability of our existence is now based on the theoretical age of the entire universe. This mathematical finding will reveal that our existence is infinitesimally improbable. However, the fact remains that at this moment (while Reet is writing, and you are reading this sentence), we all exist. All life forms (indeed all living things and all non living objects) are constrained by their respective time zones and subject to the sizes they bear in physical space. We all know about the movement of the smallest ever particles, such as the atom, and the extent of the movement of the whole universe. If we carefully pay attention to every object, we shall come to know that according to its form, each object has a different way of moving depending on its size in space. In the best illustration of this phenomenon, Reet uses the example of the longevity of certain animals, insects, and primitive life forms. For example, elephants live longer than pets; pets live longer than mosquitoes; and mosquitoes live longer than unicellular life forms, the majority of which produce offspring in a fraction of a second and die off in no time. Interestingly, the longevity in each of these cases can be correlated to the size of each of these creatures, how much space they occupy, or in some cases, the size of their internal organs. But all of them enjoy an almost equally long survival period to the time zones they are subject to within their consciousness level. In reality, all living creatures and all non-living things are only in existence now. We have no space to verify our existence in the past or the future, making us believe that only the present moment is eternally tangible. Whatever has happened in the past and whatever we anticipate happening in the future is only in our minds as impressions and projections of our creative selves.

 Concept of Universal Consciousness, Mass Consciousness, and Individual Consciousness

Reet strongly suggests that we must liberate ourselves from the convention saying that consciousness is different for different entities and that we are separate individuals, each at our level. Our consciousness primarily deals with all our physical senses and the subtler characteristics, viz. minds, intelligence, impressions, memories, behavior, and habits.

In terms of our nature, the world is just the projection made by the elements of our physical senses and subtler characteristics. Hence, Reet says that his impressions about you as a person, and about all other people, form his perspectives are responsible for his world, which one may say, in turn, is constituted by you and all others from the perspective of his familiarization.

On the other hand, your world is subject to your impressions of Reet as a person and of all other people, and your world in turn is constituted by him and all others as per your familiarization. In that case, how do Reet and you live in the same world? Despite this, the fact remains that the world is one.

When Reet considers himself to be aware of his domain of consciousness, you and all other things in this world are just a creation of his consciousness. In his domain, he chooses to interact with all others the way he wants to. Choosing may entail being limited by the choices afforded by his mind, which is under the dictatorship of his individual intelligence, impressions, memories, behaviors, and habits. The state of his mind is a blend of his intelligence, impressions, memories, behaviors, and habits. The mind, therefore, is the screen of all the events that an individual has come across in his or her life. According to Reet, your existence is simply within the domain of his consciousness; and to you, his existence is within the domain of your consciousness.

Likewise, our existences are just complementary to all that exists in this world. Hence, the existence of all things in this world, though they appear to be multiple, converges into one single entity in the hands of the undivided consciousness. To put it more simply, when Reet addresses himself, he refers to himself as 'I'. When you address yourself, you refer to yourself as 'I'. So, it goes with a third person who also addresses herself as 'I'. "So, aren't we all 'I'?", he suggests.

According to Reet, life becomes easier when we are assimilated into a single entity and no longer differentiate ourselves from all the other elements of the world. On the other hand, we are always in conflict with others who are present within our domain.

This is not only true for our relationship with the outer world but is equally applicable to the system within our anatomy which is responsible for ailments that we suffer from. We disintegrate ourselves from part of our physical bodies and then blame some foreign invader, saying it is responsible for carrying the disease to the affected body part. By the time we analyze the disease and seek to discover its cause, we enter the vicious cycle of curing the disease with medication. Medication is just thought to be the cure for a disease, but as a matter of fact we heal our disease ourselves with our firm belief in the positive results of the medicines used. We can create anything, be it a disease or good health, or anything else that we wish, but only in association with the greater force of consciousness. Take for instance the functioning of your body in a good state of health. Reet presumes that you recall the primary envelope. You feel that you have complete control over the functioning of your body organs according to your own will. It is the result of the unification process of the core consciousness of your will with the organs of your physical body, which has no distinct material link. He believes that you don't usually doubt the ability of your will to preside over the normal functioning of your physical body. The moment you doubt, the command of your will over your body organs, you start inviting ailments. So, what about in cases dealing with the outside world? Do we apply the full command of our will to our day-to-day happenings? No, we doubt every step while taking the steps. It is this attitude that invites failure, analogous to illness of our organs. From the foregoing, we gather that a person is responsible for any event that takes place in her life. She may have the same in common with another person, and that other person is completely responsible for his own experience of that event. Reet suggests that let us not bother with how you can be wholly responsible for the same act if you have that act in common with him and for which he holds himself accountable in isolation. It is just the play of the one among the whole, undoubtedly, he has total control over the act, and by acting thus, he makes things better for himself, for you, and for all the people they have in common.

This phenomenon is true of all things, all events, and all incidents that take place in this world perceived by individual consciousness. Earlier, Reet left some things unexplained relating to the birth of the child and its father's and mother's roles. He says that in the birth of a child, the child himself is fully responsible for the same attributable factors as his father and his mother, who are also responsible for his birth and wholly accountable in their respective roles in complete isolation. Another person who is affected directly and indirectly by the birth of the child is wholly responsible for the event of the birth. Likewise, you will find that the entire functioning of this world is the wish of one out of the many, further leveraging the process of evolution that is possible for humans, with the control residing at the individual level. He further explains what is required of all of us. That wc should come out of the convention of the concept of individual mindset constantly holding outside factors responsible and to take refuge in the unified consciousness for the benefit of us all.

✦ Analogy of a Monkey Fighting with His Mirror Image ✦

Reet likes a certain analogy involving a mirror that he heard from a noblewoman. A monkey happened to see his image in a mirror and assumed that there was a monkey on the other side of the mirror's surface. The monkey tried and tried to control the behavior of the other monkey and finally resorted to quarreling . He got himself hurt in the process. Poor monkey. Had he known that the other monkey was just a mere projection of himself, he could have controlled his behavior to control the behavior of the monkey in the mirror. This is like the process we undergo in reality while trying to control outside forces in our ignorance. Let's not create that which we don't want to happen to ourselves, and let's refrain from playing the blame game, which is holding an outside factor responsible for all our woes. The outside factor is just a reflection of the work of your creative self within the domain of your consciousness.

✧ Process of Materialization. Time and Space in the Context of a Conscious Entity ✧

Our instincts spontaneously produce the so-called outer environment within the domain of our consciousness. This appears to happen simultaneously with our thoughts creating our mental domain. We do this in our dreams as well as in so-called reality, but we accept it as merely the occurrence of events put into play by outside forces. This happens in the core of our consciousness, the inner etheric space, in a timeless and spaceless environment with a consistent projection of our creations to the outer environment over the mental plane as captured through a scries of thoughts. Time and space are not two separate things. Time is the space meant for your consciousness to count on the events that you create with the consolidation of your thoughts on the individual mental plane. Whereas, space is meant for the matter to support those events and provide a dimensional perspective. In other words, time and space are relative in terms of the consciousness of the individual entity, as well as the state of consciousness of the same person or entity. Time dilates and shrinks for the same person depending on the state of her consciousness and in conjunction with the pace of her thoughts within a given chronological gap. The more attention our level of consciousness pays to a hypothetical or gross event, the more the period of the event dilates, and the less attention we pay to it, the more the period in which the event occurs shrinks. One may say attention is attained with help of identical thoughts that roll through the individual mind. That is why, for what we do, we execute the work in the present moment in the eternal time frame. But when we swing between the non-existing past and future, we tend to produce uncontrolled chaotic events in our minds, inviting those incidents to the present moment, which means we are responsible for the outcome. Reet is not saying here that we should not have any plans. We must plan, but we should plan constructively in the present moment to produce the results of our choices , but without the element of doubt based on experiences of things that have hindered our works. Therefore, to avoid doubts in our execution of works is to bring about certain positive outcomes. To him , the Big Bang is an incident that has resulted in the purest form of universal consciousness coming into being in the material envelopes from the timeless and spaceless planes in the form of multiple consciousnesses playing different roles and constrained by the limitations of time and space. Therefore, he says that our every act at the individual level is, in turn, the act of the universal consciousness on the eternal plane translating its objective through the relatively narrower perspectives of the individual entities constituting mass consciousness. Our consciousness is essentially guided by our mind, with our minds playing a pivotal role in feeding the pure form of consciousness with information about the outer environment and acting to create things following the commands of consciousness. In the process, we all tend to react to the incidents we create in the outer world. But if we could reverse the process and make the starting point originate from the level of pure consciousness, and allow projection of the same to the outer world instead of reacting to the incidents which we create unknowingly at the gross level, we would be able to avoid many undesirable events created by the attributes of our minds such as failure, anger, temptation, fear, and pain. We need to understand the role of our minds in this case and use the essence of this instrument to bring about the overdue evolution of humankind. As a matter of fact, time and space are also the creation of our minds or, in mathematical language, are the function of our consciousness.

We may practice the idea of our consciousness not being contaminated by experiences, and therefore, by the thoughts of our minds, which are primarily responsible for creating the obstacles of the outer world; and precipitating more and more problems because of a shift of the energy of our consciousness towards the troubling matter. In this case, if we could avoid the shifting of the state of our consciousness and its immense potential energy, and turn it inward to create the assertiveness within ourselves to justify our action with a transparent vision of its objective, we would be in a position to accomplish almost anything in this world. We must follow our actions with a constant realization of our inner self with its potential to fulfill its objectives. Then our work would be perfect.

✧ Dynamics of Consciousness ✧

Energy, according to physics, takes two different forms: static and kinetic. Static energy is the potential form of energy, whereas kinetic energy is the same energy ruled by dynamic forces. Likewise, the form of consciousness in its utter stillness in the potential form assumes a dynamic form of multitudes permeating matter, space, and time in the form of dynamic consciousness emanating from a single entity of the supreme consciousness. In this process, the forces of dynamics become visible through the infinite senses of the consciousness from within the material envelope(s), which is subject to constant changes, guided by the dynamics of time in a multidimensional environment of space, with time and space being two distinct functions of the physical bodies, and therefore, closely interrelated with the mind. The supreme undivided consciousness remains a witness to all dynamic forces in a poised stance through its infinite sense of the material enveloping over infinite dimensions across the plane of eternity. However, this zest has created a shift in consciousness towards the segregation of the supreme and into the individual entities separated by the shape and form for playing the individual roles dictated by the consciousness from the etheric space. Hence, the awareness of the original state of consciousness is ignored in its sheer perfection towards attaining said perfection in the roles of the individual entities through the created environment of constant change, where no two conditions are ever like the same state of the individual consciousness. The conditions that the consciousness is subject to represent events. In other words, the events are the various states of consciousness. However, the sensibility of the consciousness in response to changes to the events in isolation is the mechanism guiding the factor of time to individual consciousness in a broader and purer sense. Physical time is only a reference to the variation and repetitiveness of the events on the dimensional scale. Therefore, to the state of consciousness, time is relative and does not match with the physical parameter measure of time, so time is a sheer phenomenon of the physical body of individual consciousness. But the consciousness of a discrete nature tends to act in physical time in reaction to the stimulus of experiences, and hence time, as measured by the clock, rules the consciousness in the so-called outer environment.

When we speak of the dimensions concerning the environment, we assume that consciousness is subject to certain maneuverability in relation to the events in the particular dimension. To better understand this idea, consider when you play a video game with your full attention. There occurs a shift of the consciousness from the three-dimensional environment, apparently to the two-dimensional world (if it is two-dimensional animation) by way of your effort. A shift also occurs in the maneuverability of the consciousness. This way the consciousness is capable of traversing the entire dimensional, or multidimensional environment, with the shift of its presence. Not necessarily limited to the three-dimensional view, but capable of moving beyond the perspective manifolds to realize the core of the self and its potential. There are two types of movement of consciousness: inward and outward. The outward movement of the consciousness is the shift of the consciousness towards the things, which appear in the three-dimensional environment or lower; and the anticipation of a certain outcome in the environment through the senses and emotions of the mind, and of the consciousness. The inward movement of the consciousness is the shift of the consciousness within the domain beyond the three-dimensional environment and towards a higher dimensional environment, which in spirituality is attained by meditative practice. This space is more for maneuverability as the consciousness drifts to the higher dimensional environment. We may define space as the allowance for maneuverability of the consciousness to act in the dimensional environment and the function of the number of dimensions present in the environment. In a secluded environment, when the individual entity is subject to action on its own, the environment created by the individual remains in tandem with the individual actions of the other entities in the shared environment because of the supreme act of the undivided consciousness hinged between all individual actions, and therefore all actions of the individual entities are the expression of dynamic consciousness in the material environment by way of transfer of the form of potential energy through the metaphor of kinetic movement. All forces in the material environment represent the dynamics responsible for constantly changing said environment through the materials present in it as witnessed by the consciousness. In this process, the force dynamics become attuned to the individually created selves. For an individual entity, emotions are the drivers of consciousness. Apparently, when we view an object through the physical eyes, the outline of the object is decoded through a personal identification process using the tools of emotions perceptible to our consciousness to experience an isolated environment. And this very process creates the factor of duality in the eyes of the perceiver of individual consciousness demerging itself from the universal consciousness gradually towards the metamorphosis of consciousness into sheer material objects of this universe in its material state.

✧ Process of Personification and Visualization in Cocreating the Desired Outcome ✧

In interactions with the material environment, where the self decides to create a relationship with the material environment, be it an object or any living thing, the process of establishing or creating an identity is first in line with the self's personal experiences of an identical background is reinforced by first-hand experiences. For example, when you meet a person, ideally you will be preoccupied with your ideas about the person, essentially, by judging him or her in line with your experiences with people, reinforced by the perceived behavior of the new person and prejudiced by your past notions even though you are gathering more experiences in the process. In the next meeting with the same person, more experiences will be gathered and added to the resultant impressions gathered in the prior meeting. So, the very act of personifying the person happens in your perceived ideas through subsequent meetings with that individual. If you look closely, you will see that the experiences are predominant in your interactions with the person with whom you are building the new relationship. This applies to your relationship with anything around you, be it a human or another living thing, or any non living object. The new experiences are all related to your notions of the perceived matter, correlated to your own way of judging the same based on your experiences . So, with the passing of time, things seem less thrilling for a person because of the monotony of the impressions in the bag of memories. If you forgo the experiences by discarding or rejecting them, a newness appears when you deal with the environment, which essentially is without prejudice related to your experiences and behaviors. There are natural ways of discarding memories obtained by a conscious entity, partly by sleeping and to a larger extent by being in a coma or being in the process of death when the saturation of memories happens concerning the capacity of the consciousness in its physical configuration built on the mental plane. Saturation of memories is often accompanied by pain and physical exhaustion. The shedding of memories is essential to make necessary corrections to the physical configuration of a conscious entity. Any diseases people have are essentially the memories of ailments in the consciousness gathered by first-hand experience and with subsequent impressions reinforced upon the psyche. We fall into a vicious cycle when we realize that we have taken ill, and once we establish the nature of the ailment based on experiences with other people or which we have suffered from ourselves. This vicious cycle tends to continue until the saturation level of memories is reached, at which point natural processes are required for the shedding of these memories. So discarding is very important if we are to experience the new creative side of ourselves, but how can we attain that level? Reet refers to the first chapter: we must generate our thoughts in the space of the creative psyche, essentially the space of consciousness between two thoughts which is free from the chain of material space, and from time, the space of ample opportunities. We must dwell in that space if we wish to be more creative. But all this would be accomplished if we only change our techniques and starting point. As we have learned , matter and events are the consolidation of all our physical senses with changes that happen in certain configurations, backed up by our understanding and experiences as held in the memory under a single plane of consciousness. There we must initiate the process to consolidate our senses and co create matter and events. We must do this creatively. And when Reet says creatively, he is referring to more of a proactive process by which, without having gone through the experience ourselves, we determine the desired outcome in the form of matter or events by envisioning said outcome without the material proof in place. The starting point of the creative process is to use the technique of visualizing the desired outcome, which enables matter to precipitate, and which may be a sequential transition. This is the automatic process to use to create the desired event by default. To become free from ailments, visualize health by intensely utilizing all your senses to recall a healthy state you experienced at some earlier stage of your life. This brings relief in the initial rounds, but because of habit one normally returns to the stage of sickness. With repeated effort, this technique will bring permanent relief. We need our creative selves to be more active for children, too. Instead of asking them to score higher on an examination by putting in hard work, inculcate in them the habit of seeing the desired outcome by way of intense visualization with the use of all the physical senses. When somebody does this, it amounts to an act of communication between the etheric space and the individual consciousness on the eternal plane, where the results of the desired outcome are assured. This will enable the child to follow through with the actions needed to attain the desired outcome in the dimensional time frame.

One may make a humble beginning in undertaking this sort of practice exercise in many areas. For example, to look younger and rejuvenated, use the same technique as above. Try to feel the vigor you once experienced at some stage of your life by using intense visualization, inducing your senses to recreate your earlier appearance and rejuvenate you. This must be a repeated effort, though. It is not necessary to visualize yourself at an earlier stage. You can also visualize a new stage while creating. For example, a good number of people in this world are already experts at creating new ailments. To secure a professional position in your chosen career or a position in a certain social circle, or to become affluent, use similar exercises, but be consistent with a focused effort. You will find that the situation which earlier on you had regarded as a hindrance to your progress turns in your favor now. Visualization, engaging all your physical senses, amounts to the consolidation of the senses to precipitate the matter and is a creative step towards your desired outcome.

Beating the panic-demic

Reet is sharing an incident in his life that happened after he came back from China after an official assignment to Dalian city in November2019. On his week-long stay in Dalian, literally, he felt it as chilling as it could be during the coldest days of December in places elsewhere like Delhi.

The following day when he went to the office from his home after he came back from China, in the afternoon he received a call from my wife Liza. She said that she wasn't keeping well and was feeling feverish. He asked her not to worry since this might be because of the sudden changes in the weather condition.

That day he got back home a little earlier than the usual time from the office and found her with a moderate fever. His daughter, Anaya, who was in standard sixth also got back from her school meantime and apparently not seemed happy to be seeing her mom in that state.

That evening, soon after they had dinner together, Liza complained of uneasiness in breathing associated with body temperature more than normal. Reet said to her that this might be because of the suffocation she was feeling due to switching from the blower of the AC duct, which he deliberately put off because of the onset of winter cold in the city of his employment.

At night, they went to bed a little earlier than the usual time. Fever was not much troubling her that night as he made her consume the painkiller prescribed earlier to his daughter by the doctor a few months back.

The next morning it seemed all ok with her, but post noon she again complained of little dizziness and Reet decided to take her for a visit to the doctor But she refused, telling him that she would be feeling better over a couple of days

That sounded to him quite convincing due to his individual impression about the human body which is capable of healing itself by its potentials that normally we do not tend to realize, but if we genuinely want to feel better, in that case, we just can do that using the power of belief.

The next day, when she didn't seem to have the signs of any improvements and was consistently suffocating, Reet applied a cool pack of cotton soaked with ice on her forehead in an attempt to lower her body temperature.

In the meantime, Reet also felt it a bit feverish. They had to order food as they were not able to cook anything at home. Anaya had as usual kept all by their sides throughout the time all along.

The following day, both of them had gone to the doctor, and they came back with medicines prescribed by the doctor of a painkiller and an antibiotics course for a week. All that they were told was that they had viral fever, which at least is likely to last for a week.

The strangest thing that Reet had experienced after he came back home was a kind of vertigo,which he said that he had never come across typically whenever he had any fever on earlier occasions.

"But this is not desirable!" He spoke to himself. Indeed, he never wants to suffer from any of this kind of illness and always wants to be getting well magically in no time, out of his habitual instincts. However, he consumed medicines as prescribed by the doctor and had just been sitting in the living room while Liza was resting on the bed in the adjacent room with no sign of significant recovery from her state.

While Reet kept thinking about whether it was possible to rebuild his state of wellness in no time. Whether he could trick himself to the state of wellness by emulating wellness using his gross senses like the conditions while he was completely free from the feelings of sickness just over two days back.

He got seated deep down in his inner consciousness and witnessed each of the physical senses of visuals, auditory, smells, taste, and touch. And he was trying to figure out where exactly he had the troubles being felt by the illness that he was through, by evaluating each of his senses. Reet didn't know that this would have a remarkable sign of possibilities for recovery in that process. He could realize that all were happening exactly in the manner he was anticipating for an outcome right at that moment.

To be simpler, the state of illness and wellness from your own perspective do not have distinct differences in terms of individual physical senses. But the inclination of an individual to fall sick by anticipation in response to the individual's knowledge of the clinical phenomenon in infection, has a substantial influence on human psychology.

The process of emulating wellness using physical senses is a form of a subtle exercise in the simulation of the conditions of the state of wellness within the domain of individual consciousness against all odds outside. However, Reet just was using my gross senses to feel in the manner when it was in a state of wellness, sometimes back over a couple of days before.

And it so happened that he was able to have a full recovery from the feelings of sickness, within two days of a time. He made it a point to finish the course of antibiotics without fail. But his point is, had the incident taken place after a couple of months, he is sure this could have come as clear as COVID-19 because of the discovery of the dreaded virus, and subsequent inventions of scientifically proven methodologies for testing of the same. And his wife, who suffered for about ten days, no doubt would have landed up in the hospital for consequences as seen commonly these days.

In that period, it was not seen in any other places when it started emerging in China only from December 2019 and Reet traveled to China a month before that. Post-facto analysis on the possibility of anyone escaping the infection is completely ruled out if somebody traveled through Mainland China via airports of Shanghai, Beijing, as well as Dalian, itself, in the advent of any such dreaded virus. When COVID-19 was still unheard of, Reet and his wife suffered similar symptoms without reasons to believe otherwise, had that been a few months later with the growing awareness of people's understandability of the pandemic and with the knowhow of the inherent nature of the deadly virus.

Even in December 2019, Reet traveled back to the place of domicile and met up with almost all his friends, relatives, brothers, and their families and most importantly his parents. Despite all his sufferings and of his wife, he has no claim in saying that ever he was infected by the COVID-19 virus. Asymptomatic initially for a while and later had his wife infected with all justifiable symptoms together with him , due to the circumstances of the time when the presence of the virus was not discovered with all possible tools for diagnosis.

However, Reet's main takeaways from this incident of life: - State of panic makes all the difference for the same sickness among different persons or even in the same person depending on the prevailing situation. The consequences of any disease all depends on how one deals with the situation and physical conditions psychologically. Else, his case would have escalated to a typical case of the COVID-19 period, had the timing been deferred by a couple of months. But all Reet had applied was a restrained behavior while dealing with his sickness without the associated anxieties of the times, because of complete ignorance.

- The capacity of building up resistance and self-healing is one of the key takeaways. Tackling the same with the use of gross physical senses emulating the conditions of wellness is a wonderful tool for a person. One must genuinely desire to have established the mental capacity empowerment to think against all odds and be opportune to anticipate things we desire against existing conditions and preconditions. Reet got himself healed in two days, and he genuinely wanted back his state of wellness, and so with exercise, he undertook simulating the conditions of wellness. His simple idea is why should he think of himself falling victim to something undesirable and clinging to the idea of falling sick by emulating the state of illness instead.

- We all need to stay away from all unnecessary information, which nowadays represents another form of hazard that may be coined as information hazard—to prevent panic and beat the influence of the pandemic.

So, Reet suggests that let us all "Beat the Panic-demic" by saving as many lives on earth through spreading the essence of the story, while keeping everybody on this earth safer, healthier, and happier forever.

Additionally, Reet wants to make clear to the readers that he doesn't even remotely suggest to anybody for improper behavior as excuses to bypass the COVID-19 protocols & laws/bylaws, thereof; and any medical treatment recommended by the approved medical practitioners in this regard.

✣ Breaking of an Ice ✣

Professor Krishnan on the day of the meeting with Reet had shared a real story with him about a management student, which Krishnan always kept as a trump card in explaining the power of self and using a unique concept for exploring the self.

"Perform as if nobody is watching you and wait for the magic to happen." Prithvi didn't much understand what Ma'am Reeta had advised him after the group discussion round, in response to his personal request for her advice outside the hall. He was very upset since he must clear his management papers for the last semester, and he couldn't do well in the group discussion, which is going to be graded. Prithvi knows that he has trouble speaking out clearly in public, but it didn't really work out despite his incessant efforts to break the ice. Prithvi who is aiming at a job soon after completing his post-graduate management degree has developed unseen anxiety over recent times due to his inability to overcome his limitations. He is going to appear in the series of campus interviews by some renowned companies/ corporate houses with other students of his batch, scheduled over the following months. Although, Prithvi prefers Crystal Solutions over all other companies visiting the campus, but he has been squeezed into a state *of* hopelessness being humbled by his peer group in the private discussions which he overheard accidentally in the classroom with types of remarks about him like, "Beggars can't be choosers". He considers himself not bad in most of the subjects of the management curriculum. He thinks that most of his friends have the distinct edge over him of their innate abilities to speak uninhibitedly in front of the interviewers, which may outshine him from others in the selection process for jobs; thought that has left him terribly despaired these days. Prithvi has decided to gather help from Ma'amReeta in this regard to know more about her opinion, especially more he is interested in knowing about the magic that she spoke of. In the afternoon when he came back to the hostel after attending ORT with Professor Jamal, he called up Ma'am Reeta on her mobile while walking the hostel corridor on his way to the room, but Ma'am Reeta didn't pick up the call. "Hey Prithvi, are you playing TT, I bet you would like my new skill in tackling the spin," Yogen spoke to Prithvi when he came running from behind and left him hurriedly. "Nope, buddy! I have important work to do." Prithvi responded and walked just behind him down the corridor. "Ok, no prob buddy. Just join my party in the evening. You will find me still playing." Yogen spoke with enthusiasm. Yogen has a bright chance in clicking interviews as he has higher grades in all papers in the earlier semesters, including his trait of outspoken character. Prithvi entered his room in the hostel , and he went for a shower directly in the washroom. When he came back, he traced the call from Ma'am Reeta on his mobile that he left on the bed. He was expecting Ma'am Reeta to respond, as she is known for her generosity in helping her students. He promptly called her back and fixed an appointment with her in her office for the next day in the morning. Furthermore, he felt so happy to be able to get the appointment from Ma'am Reeta for obvious reasons. "Good morning, ma'am !" Prithvi greeted ma'am Reeta in her office the following day. Ma'am Reeta acknowledged Prithvi by greeting him back. She was busy doing something on her laptop. She asked Prithvi to have a seat in front of her desk with her implied gesture. "Prithvi, it would take a few minutes to complete my task. I hope you won't mind." Ma'am Reeta asked Prithvi, apologetically, but Prithvi assured her that he had no inconvenience as his final semester classes are all nearing completion except for a few, and the only class for Organization was scheduled in the latter part of the day. So, he was not in a hurry. But as a matter of fact, Prithvi anxiously was waiting for Ma'am Reeta to speak out of the magic she said to him the other day. "Yes, Prithvi, how can I help you?" Ma'am Reeta asked Prithvi with a warm smile after a few minutes coupled with a sense of little seriousness towards his concern which was explicitly appearing on his face. "Ma'am , I need your help. Yesterday you told me about some tips to improve my performance, but I was not able to get that. Can you kindly elaborate?" Prithvi responded a little hesitantly. Ma'am Reeta had her laptop set aside towards the corner of the desk and started speaking out to Prithvi. "Look, Prithvi. I can share with you a wonderful tip in overcoming your limitation, which I personally am a user myself, and it is absolutely useful. Yesterday, when I observed you participating in the group discussion, you held back your words despite your intent in participating in the discussion. You appeared inhibited and reserved throughout the entire session of the discussions. By seeing you, I was reminded of myself and my helplessness in the past. I also faced the same troubles as yours, back in my school days. So do not worry, you will be able to overcome your limitations." Prithvi was very happy to receive the words of assurance from Ma'am Reeta. She continued further, "But I just won't share this with everyone as every other person doesn't really deserve this kind of education. For you as well, I highly recommend you to follow my tips with absolute care and conviction." "Alright, Ma'am. I would love to know about the tip from you and assure you that I shall practice it hard." Prithvi responded with more interest because he doesn't want to leave any stone unturned in his effort to break free from his utter distress. Ma'am Reeta felt obliged to tell Prithvi about the tip on his assurance, and she continued further "Prithvi, as you will be able to understand that our acts are all engaging opinions of others or in anticipation of opinions inviting judgments by others. When this happens, your focus splits partly into the work you attempt, and a major chunk of your attention runs behind recognition by others. My tip is just to bring back the entire focus on your work, leaving aside what others think. But how to negate the judgments and recognition by others on your work; and bring back your entire focus in the effort alone. This can be accomplished." "This can be accomplished if you start practicing the art of Unit-versal mind which says that only a single mind is real for the performer which is of our own, but minds of all others are just manifestations of expressions in anticipation. Others showing up opining judging your performance do not exist in your domain unless you take their opinions and judgments for granted by your interpretation and inferences. So, you need to be careful and do not fall back on the opinions formed by others because they do not really exist. Once you establish your opinion as more important than all others, things would be more productive for you. If you can negate opinions formed by others, you will be performing extraordinarily." Ma'am Reeta continued after a pause, staring at Prithvi in his eyes. "Tell me how it would be if you work in a secluded environment and nobody observes you. Suppose one Mr. Dan is good at dancing . But generically speaking, why Mr. Dan can perform at home, but he is so hesitant to display his skills in front of the crowds. For instance, you are very good at writing but if anybody follows you when you write, wouldn't that be troubling you? To change the habit of inhibition, you have to understand the concept of the Unit-versal mind, which works like magic." Prithvi had leaned back relaxed in the chair, drawing in more comfort to his posture, and kept listening to Ma'am Reeta with utmost attention with folded hands over the desk. He never realized that he will get to hear something out of the box from Ma'am Reeta as he engages all the time with his genuine intent and effort to overcome his limitation, and this, the concept of the Unit-versal mind had really signaled something altogether different from all his earlier learnings to overcome limitations. Prithvi recalled last year's sports day, where he fell short of his usual skills playing TT to his opponent Ritesh for a defeat straight in the first three rounds. He earlier defeated Ritesh on ample occasions when they played TT in the hostel against each other. Ma'am Reeta's line of discussion is enlightening for Prithvi to understand that he has fallen on the habit of replicating his ingrained behavior even in his favorite sports for being cowed down by focusing more on people and surroundings. Prithvi got all the answers, but he never had thought of such ideas. He enquired back to Mam Reeta. "It is absolutely a solution for a lifetime Mam, but how should I practice the concept?" She felt no discomfort in responding to him as she knew that this would be a little challenging for somebody like Prithvi who by far is an introverted character. However, this would not limit Prithvi in overcoming the problem as he appears to have a genuine urge to change himself, and Ma'am Reeta asked him a little trickily." "Prithvi, how come a reserved person like you is asking me questions at the moment with so much of comfort when in classes you have never been able to speak a word in front of the other faculties." Prithvi said, "Ma'am, you are far more accommodating, that's why." Ma'am Reeta said,"That's where you are being tricked. You look for someone to support your views, your queries. But just imagine a person, for instance, Professor Jamal in my place. Your behavior will instantly change in consideration of the impression you normally carry about the person. And that's where you must work, just follow what you ought to communicate, not focusing on what people would be judging you out of your act. You can't enter anybody's mind wondering what he thinks, but invariably you use your mind interpreting another person's mind and gestures in so many ways." Ma'amReeta continued after a pause "Even nature doesn't allow you to enter into the minds of others. So, who are you to judge what another person thinks just by their mere expressions and gestures? Just create what you want out of this life, judge yourself and judge your instincts instead of judging all others on what they think. The Unit-versal mind teaches you to be focused on your mind throughout by following what you think. The moment you are anticipating an undesired outcome, you must quickly work in your mind to change the focus to an outcome you desire and feel with a higher degree of intensity using all your gross senses." The discussion with Madam Reeta brought a great sense of relief to Prithvi. He felt a genuine comfort for what he had got from Madam Reeta. "Wisdom is worth millions of conventional ideas." Prithvi recounts in his mind silently. He felt so thankful to her that he said to her, "Ma'am, I am so much indebted to you. Perhaps, my problems have ended from today with your wisdom, which has made me realize that I am the creator of my troubles." Ma'am Reeta said back to Prithvi, "Practice the Unit-versal mind, which stands for single unit mind blended with Universal intelligence and that is the mind which you must possess." Prithvi fell no short of his effort in assuring Madam Reeta that he would be committed to practicing the Unit-versal Mind, felt extremely grateful to her while leaving, carrying all his way the delights of a bird freed from the captivated cage. Prithvi when he went back walking from Ma'am Retta's office, strongly felt like having a cup of coffee in the campus cafeteria. He called his father Sanjay from his mobile while sipping on his cup of coffee, "Hey Dad I clicked my interview with Crystal Solutions. It's just a matter of time now." Sanjay technically understood what his son meant and didn't bother much with what he had meant. Instead, he asked him, "How is madam Reeta? It sounds like she has been helpful. I was telling you earlier many times that nothing is wrong with you, but you have given up hopes. I am glad that you have gained back your courage. By the way, son. Your mother is planning for a trip to Europe after you come back home after completing your exams. What about you? Are you going to join us for the trip?" "No worries, Dad. You proceed with mom. No more shall I spend your money from now as I know that I am going to qualify for my interview and join a job soon. All that I wish that I could take you and mom together for another pleasure trip to a hill station in India after you come back from Europe with my own money.", said Prithvi chuckling. Sanjay laughed out happily and blessed his son. He was so pleased to be able to find his son gaining his self-confidence as he genuinely understands his problem from childhood. He didn't bother to find out how he had managed the three-sixty-degree turn in his perception about his ability, and he even was not concerned about whether Prithvi was joining a job sooner or later. But he was happy because Sanjay had realized that this time his son, Prithvi, had broken the ice.

55

✦ Concept of Evolved Unit-versal Mind ✦

Reet suggests that this is an evolutionary concept of a conscious entity, which he learned from the discussion with Professor Krishnan when he told the story about Prithvi. The fact remains that we have no access to any person's mind. The barrier is created with some purpose to rationalize the fact that everything in the so-called outside world is your interpretation and the analysis of your mind. The Unit-versal mind stands for universal mind together with a single-unit mind. If you are dedicated to conceptualizing, this will afford you ample opportunities. Moreover, this we must attain for the sake of the next stage of the evolution of humankind. Now imagine if you were given a platform where no one is observing your acts. The dimension of your freedom would be far-reaching, and you would be more creative in a sense. But in gross reality one cannot have this kind of freedom as the acts of an individual are constrained by multiple entities and their observations. Yet again, this is not true. Nobody really observes you, except for your ideas about being observed by others. And you are making yourself a victim out of all these ideas for an entirely unseen reason in the process of individualizing yourself. To be precise, it is prudent to stay away from what exists in the minds of others since in your domain of reality such things are nonexistent until and unless you recognize and analyze things from your point of view, projecting into the minds of others. All news on the air, which you are influenced by in gross reality, is simply the work of your mind in reaction to some elementary material evidence that is fugitive and temporary to a large extent. Just so you understand, our creativity leads to situations irrespective of whether the situation is controlled or uncontrolled. A situation is a function of our mind, and we can use the mind to create prosperity and helplessness, and anything in between. To seclude our mind from anything it simulates, we must be observant of our thoughts and the chain such observation creates out of those thoughts.

Most of our thoughts revolve around the thoughts of others in the struggle for attention or recognition or any other form of expectation. But we must understand that this has no meaning since we have no tool to gauge the minds of others except through evidence that is available to the analysis exercised by your own mind. Let us look at an instance from daily life. Somebody, X, said to you that your best friend, Y, has a very bad opinion about you, which he divulged to Mr. X confidentially. Since Mr. X is your well-wisher, he expressed the matter to you in order to be safe in dealing with Mr. Y in the future . Now, this is the point where you start analyzing, asking why on earth Y has such an opinion about you. In the process of analyzing, the reasons keep springing out, and you finally establish the reasons by your own creative self. Another way of dealing with this is through observing all the thoughts which emanated from your mind when you were told about the statement of Y by Mr. X. And you start putting aside those thoughts so as not to disturb your state of mind at the present stage and nullify the effects by choosing not to react. If you are able to find a way out of that decision, sooner or later all factors will disappear and be dissolved in your domain without any sort of external exercise that people normally resort to, to convince others of the views in their minds. This will happen since you believe without a doubt that you are free from what apparently goes on in others' minds. This exercise should be adhered to even in the worst situation you go through. See the amazing results that your creative psyche brings forth in order to change the conditions in no time by your belief and trust in the Unit-versal mind concept. This concept has been created because of sharing experiences by adopting the exercise of the Unit-versal mind to be helped out of all difficulties and despair and, instead, to empower yourself in a new dimension with all resources available given your context and your needs.

✦ The Phrase "Operated from Within" ✦

Reet says that this is a beautiful pathway where all your worries and your suffering are gone, and you are one with the consciousness to choose your own. Summary of the points discussed by Reet in "Life Operated from Within":

1. Never contaminate the psyche with unwanted thoughts. The mind is your subtlest organ, which rules all your actions and the outcomes of those actions. The moment you feed something in your mind with the aid of thought and analysis, check whether you desire the inevitable outcome. If the outcome is desirable, then proceed as planned, but if it is not, don't proceed as planned. If despite your efforts, you are unable to control your mind, transfer the responsibility immediately to the inner space of consciousness and refuse to further entangle it with thought. The effort may result in secondary thoughts further on in the process, so keep on transferring the responsibility towards the unseen until the end.

2. It is essential to be sincere in your senses. Retain the spontaneous energy form of the consciousness and try to experience all the outer happenings in the inner world. You know that impulses in the outer environment are the creation of your inner consciousness. For example, if you hear something. Don't make use of your senses to reach out towards the noise in the outer environment, but rather, feel the sound as the creation of your consciousness using the tool or instrument called your body. You can apply this to all your senses, and thus will become aware of the one within you who remains as a witness to all these senses, in full control

of the happenings, including control over time. In other words, this is analogous to meditative practice in that you are keeping yourself in the present moment, which is eternally real. Thus, you operate from within.

3. Consider that the present moment is real and is worth living up to objectively. The past is a hallucination populated by impermanent and fugitive events. How you handle the present moment determines the past and similarly the future, which conventionally falls into the pattern of the past hallucinated behavior of an individual. Do not dwell in the mind. When we dwell in the mind, we tend to swing between the past and the future and are ruled by doubts and uncertainties. Mind you, only the present moment is real, and only the present moment can fetch you all the material needed for happiness. In other words, believe without a doubt in anything you do. This is only possible if you remain present in the present moment. Doubt creates duality, and duality creates difficulties.

4. Creation happens in the domain beyond the dimension of time and space. Whereas , time and space support the material evidence of the outcome of that which you have created. The mind of the spirit grabs elements of the imprinted past by experiencing things in time and space and brings forth the ingredients for creating things by way of the spirit in the timeless and spaceless domain, bringing to the next level of materialization things and events characterized by time and space, and so this process continues like a chain reaction. On the other hand, the response to the outcome becomes reactive and impulsive according to the individual's experiences and is repetitive in a sense. The reactive nature of what you create, however, can be avoided by creating new conditions which are free from precedent, that is, any prior events and any material outcome. For instance, there is a gap between two thoughts where a conscious entity is free from the constraint of time and space. Becoming aware of this gap, unaffected by any thought, renders the opportunities to create things that are independent of all past events. Therefore, your present handling of the moment even has the potential to figuratively mend your past.

5. Every appearance of a material entity can now be retrieved for its history, with its inference to the mind engaged in logical sequences. The past does not necessarily have to precede the manifestation of matter and events in the present context, but rather the present circumstances result in a retrieval of the past subjective positions. This affords ample opportunities for an individual entity to mend the situation at will.

6. A conscious entity is an eternal being. The age of the universe vis-à-vis the present moment of the conscious observer shows that the existence of the entity is highly improbable. But despite this fact, the existence of the conscious entity in the form of an observer in the present moment supports the fact of the eternal existence of the self.

7. Consciousness is an etheric substance and the center of all creation, including the subtler attributes of the physical presence, viz. mind, body, and intelligence. It is analogous to a mirror in that it reflects all objects in the universe and is instrumental in realizing and protecting them.

8. Always look within. Be in self-awareness mode. All other characters are only puppets playing different roles within the domain of your consciousness. If you are in control of yourself, concerning your mind, you will have full control over all others and that is guaranteed. There is only one mindset that rules. There are no multiple rulers for any given condition within the dimensions of time and space. All expressions and manifestations are deciphered from the outer environment through a single mind that appears as multiples.

9. Accept all events and all characters without prejudice regarding their characteristics and implications. Remain in the stance you prefer without being affected by these events and characters. Don't allow your mind to intervene because things, which are in any way the same, but are often colored as per our likes and dislikes if we allow our mind to intrude and analyze the situation and the condition.

Technique: Always let your attitude of unconditional goodwill prevail, in all places, and towards all characters and events.

10. Never, ever quarrel with the elements of your consciousness. This is the best guideline to follow if you wish to glide over all obstacles in life. The elements of our consciousness are anything that we can perceive, sense, and/or think. Heal yourself from all your ailments and troubles by applying this rule. This means that you should not be opposed to anything.

11. Dump your petty attributes like ego, jealousy, lust, greed, idleness, anger, and any other attributes based on your individual needs and taste because these attributes act as a hindrance to your holistic purpose of being united with the higher consciousness and leveraging all control at his command. Look for the most powerful and most fulfilling possession instead of these petty possessions.

12. Begin your day with twenty minutes of meditation. For the first five minutes, witness all your thoughts. Then the following five minutes, shed your thoughts by pampering yourself. The next five minutes, witness yourself sitting behind the veil, then for the last five minutes, completely surrender to the inner space of your consciousness. Ideally, during this time, you will see that your consciousness is free from all materialistic thoughts, that it is the manifestation of the higher consciousness, and that this is the merging process. You may continue to experience these feelings of self-realization during the workday. This makes all things perfect.

13. Go beyond the limitations of your mind by taking refuge in the Unit-versal intelligence.

14. Never, ever fear. To fear is to invite trouble before it exists.

15. Nothing in the outer environment is absolute. There are no parameters for length. Time and heat are not absolutes but rather are approximations concerning the state of consciousness. If consciousness is realized to the core, the physical attributes are at a loss for their ways of measuring things, and in such a circumstance the smallest things in the environment may appear monstrous. The measures of diseases are also to be regarded with skepticism and are not absolute. Take for instance diabetes and hypertension, which have numerical attributes for measurement of the parameters established by medical science. Once one falls prey to the parameters which are indicated beyond the normal range, the imprints are seated deeply in the mind, inviting a vicious cycle of disease. Absoluteness is the overall call of all the attributes of the state of consciousness and a summation of all the attributes over the present moment. So how is this overall absoluteness fragmented by assigning importance to the attributes in the case of an individual in his psyche, leading his way into suffering or out of suffering?

16. Time and space are functions of the physical senses. They are the creations of the individual conscious entity attained through the material body, in which the expansion of the consciousness is realized by consolidating the physical senses to create the material body (the primary envelope to achieve the first stage of expansion of the consciousness). Subsequently, consciousness assumes a physical state and starts expanding in the created space (the secondary envelope of consciousness) to interact with the material environment. The movement realized by the mind of consciousness in space for its sequence of separate events is registered as time in the process of expansion by keeping track of the odd events and material repetitive in nature.